Published in the UK in 2016 by Short Books
Unit 316, ScreenWorks,
22 Highbury Grove, London N5 2ER

10 9 8 7 6 5 4 3 2 1

Copyright © 2016 Short Books

Published in association with Verlagsgruppe Droemer Knaur GmbH

Illustrations © Shutterstock
Except 52 & 78 by Two Associates
And select illustrations by Short Books

A CIP catalogue record for this book is available from the
British Library.

ISBN 978-1-78072-287-0

Printed and bound in Great Britain by
CPI Group (UK) Ltd, Croydon, CR0 4YY

Cover design by Two Associates

101 THINGS
TO DO WHEN YOU'RE NOT DRINKING

ROBERT SHORT

Introduction

If you're reading this then you've noticed it too. Wherever you go, our society seems to be built around alcohol.

Whether it's boozy corporate lunches, winding down with a glass of wine, or getting together with friends at the pub – having a drink has become central to our lives. But does it mean we are missing out on other things?

Let's change the record and get creative with our time again. The activities in this book will help you clear the fog and rediscover life fresh-faced and care free.

1.

Write a list of the three things you're going to buy with the money you've saved from not drinking:

Treat Yourself

1 ....
....

2 ....
....

3 ....
....

2.

Host a
games night.

Instead of "bring
a bottle", this is a
**"bring a board
game"party.**

From **backgammon
tournaments** to
**Trivial Pursuit
showdowns,**

anything goes.

3.

Learn how to count to ten in Japanese.

一　二　三
one　two　three
ichi　ni　san

四　五　六　七
four　five　six　seven
shi　go　roku　shichi

八　九　十
eight　nine　ten
hachi　kyuu　juu

4.

Recapture the joys of childhood.

Go to your local
children's playground
and have a go on the
zip line or swings.

5.

Create a tagline for a movie about your life:

Who would you choose to play:

You

Your best friend

Your nemesis

Your first love

6.

Pick up the phone right now and call someone you've been meaning to speak to for ages.

Go on, dial now, before you turn the page!

7.

Try these conversation ice breakers for sober socialising:

If you could travel through time which way would you go, backwards or forwards?

What song would you choose for the theme tune of your life?

What makes you laugh when you're alone?

8.

Which puzzle piece can you rotate to fit into the empty space?

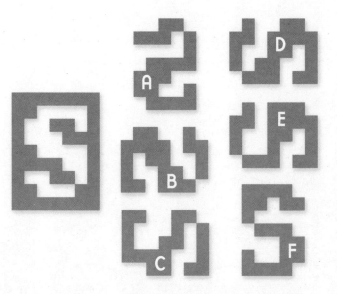

9.

Take a night walk with friends.

Instead of staggering home in the dark after one too many, plan a nocturnal journey and enjoy noticing the way your local area changes when the sun goes down.

10.

Take advantage of your clear head to improve your memory.

Look at the faces and names below. Memorise which names go with which faces.

David

Theresa

Jeremy

Hillary

Michael

Andrea

Nigel

Angela

Donald

11.

Master this yoga pose:

Shavasana

Lie on your back and open out your arms to 45 degrees.

Breathe slowly and deeply through your nose.

Allow your body to soften into the ground.

Benefits:
- The ultimate relaxation tool.
- Easily adaptable from a common drinker's position.

12.

Make a list of three things
you'll get done on those
long Sunday mornings:

Action List

1 ....

....

....

2 ....

....

....

3 ....

....

....

13.

Dig an old wine bottle out of the recycling and make a bottle-top candle.

14.

Write a story which includes these four things.

15.

Grow a plant from seed.

16.

Hold your own dry film festival.

Gather friends together for
a collection of films around
a chosen theme.

(Anything from early Russian cinema to
recent Spiderman incarnations will do.)

17.

Open a recipe book on a random page and make whatever you find there.

18.

Design your own tattoo:

19.

Can you put names to the faces from activity #10?

...How did you do?

Try this trick to improve your name recall:

1. When you're told a name, repeat it and think of something the name reminds you of.
2. Pick out the most distinctive feature on that person's face and link that to whatever it was the name brought to mind.
3. Next time you see the face, the feature will prompt the name.

e.g. Nigel "needs gel" for his moustache.

Now go back to activity #10 and try again.

20.

Declutter

...and make money at the same time by doing a bootsale. (You'll have to get up early but that won't be hard without the hangover!)

21.

Feel virtuous:
Work out how many calories
you are saving by not drinking.

Here's a rough guide:

1 pint of lager	=	197 calories
1 pint of cider	=	216 calories
175ml glass of wine	=	160 calories
A glass of champagne	=	89 calories
A margarita	=	120 calories
A gin & tonic	=	110 calories
A shot of whisky	=	105 calories

22.

Fill your usual "drinking times" with other things:

At 6.30pm

Instead of going to the pub after work, meet a close friend for coffee and a chat.

At 8.00pm

Instead of cracking open a bottle of wine, make your own detox drink.

Add chunks of cucumber and lemon to a jug of water and let it infuse overnight.

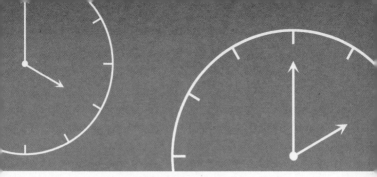

At 10.00pm

Instead of rolling in from the pub, Have an early night.

Getting enough sleep (for an adult that's between 7 to 9 hours a night) can affect your mental and physical wellbeing. So catch some extra zzzs while you can.

23.

Watch an online university lecture on a subject that's always interested you.

24.

Write down three things you used to love doing but stopped when you started drinking.

1 ....

....

2 ....

....

3 ....

....

What's stopping you now...?

25.

"Say what you see"
to work out these Rebus
visual word puzzles:

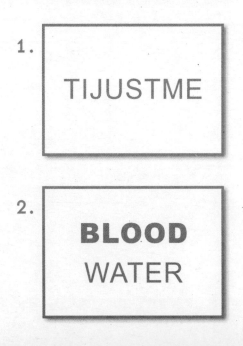

1. TIJUSTME

2. **BLOOD**
WATER

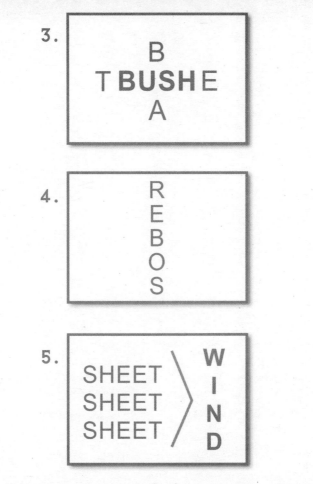

3.

B
T **BUSH** E
A

4.

R
E
B
O
S

5.

SHEET
SHEET   W
SHEET   I
          N
          D

Answers over the page

Rebus Puzzle Solutions:

1. Just in time

2. Blood is thicker than water

3. Beat around the bush

4. Sober up

5. Three sheets to the wind

26.

Become a morning person.

27.

Settle in for a box set marathon.

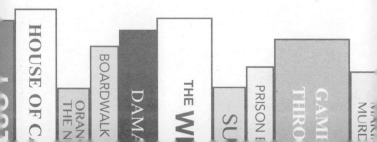

1947
1948
1949
1950
1951
1952
1953
1954
1955
1956
1957
1958
1959
1960

43
44
45
46
47
48
49
50
51
52
53
54
55
56
57

28.

Go for a
walk with
one of your
parents or
grandparents
and ask them
to tell you
about their
childhood.

29 Look up at the stars.
Can you spot these constellations?

Taurus, the bull

Perseus

Andromeda

Cassiopeia

Pegasus,
the winged horse

Cepheus

Cygnus, the swan

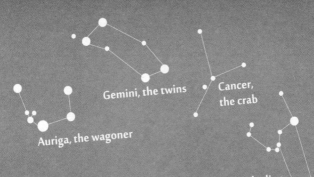

Gemini, the twins

Cancer,
the crab

Auriga, the wagoner

Leo, the lion

Pole Star,
the north star

Ursa Major,
the great bear

Ursa Minor,
the little bear

Hercules

Corona Borealis,
the northern crown

Lyra, the lyre

30.

Can you match up the historical speeches with their key quote opposite?

1. Emmeline Pankhurst, "Freedom or Death"
13 November 1913

2. Winston Churchill, "Their Finest Hour"
18 June 1940

3. Margaret Thatcher, "Britain Awake"
19 January 1976

4. Nelson Mandela, address to the 49th session of the General Assembly
3 October 1994

5. Bill Clinton, speech to journalists during impeachment inquiry
11 December 1998

Answers: 1c, 2a, 3d, 4e, 5b

a) "Of this I am quite sure, that if we open a quarrel between the past and the present, we shall find that we have lost the future."

b) "So nothing, not piety, nor tears, nor wit, nor torment can alter what I have done. I must make my peace with that."

c) "I dare say, in the minds of many of you - you will perhaps forgive me this personal touch - that I do not look either very like a soldier or very like a convict, and yet I am both."

d) "Let's ensure that our children will have cause to rejoice that we did not forsake their freedom."

e) "However hard the battle will be, we will not surrender. Whatever the time it will take, we will not tire."

31.

Recite the alphabet backwards.

32.

I taste a liquor never brewed –
From Tankards scooped in Pearl –
Not all the Frankfort Berries
Yield such an Alcohol!

Inebriate of air - am I -
And Debauchee of Dew -
Reeling - thro' endless summer days -
From inns of molten Blue -

When "Landlords" turn the drunken Bee
Out of the Foxglove's door –
When Butterflies – renounce their "drams" –
I shall but drink the more!

Emily Dickinson

33.

Throw a mocktail party.

Invite your friends over and tell them to get dressed up — then play barman, creating weird and wonderful alcohol-free cocktails.

Not Quite Piña Colada

- 2 ripe bananas (frozen)
- 340g of pineapple chunks
- 240ml non-sweetened pineapple juice
- 200ml coconut milk (made into frozen cubes in an ice-cube tray)
- Coconut flakes to garnish

Put all the ingredients in a blender and blitz until smooth. Pour into cocktail glasses and sprinkle with coconut flakes.

...Enjoy!

34.

Pick three topics that make you angry enough to start a blog:

Angry Blog Ideas

1 ....
....
....

2 ....
....
....

3 ....
....
....

35.

You could start writing now:

My First Blog Post

36.

Buy a bunch of

flowers

for yourself

and put them

somewhere

where they'll

make you smile

Join a local

37

sports team

38.

Exercise the executive function of your frontal lobe with this puzzle.

What number should appear in the empty triangle?

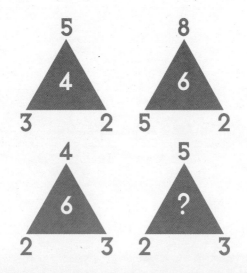

Do a music swap. Do a music swap.

39

Discover some new music
by trading five album
recommendations with a friend.

40.

Test your sobriety by reciting this tongue twister:

Any noise annoys an oyster, but a noisy noise annoys an oyster most.

41.

Now devise your own tongue twister to test out your friends...

42.

Try this walking
meditation.

1. Walk at a slow, comfortable pace and focus on your feet.

2. Notice the moment your heel touches the ground and the roll of the ball of your foot as you move onto your toes.

3. Notice the feeling of your shoes, your socks and any little aches or pains.

4. Try to stop your mind wandering by repeatedly bringing your focus back to your feet.

P.S. Look where you're going!

43.

Pull some shapes at a roller disco.

44.

Write down the rest of the poem from activity #32 without turning back to look at it:

I taste a liquor never brewed –

From Tankards scooped in Pearl –

Inebriate of air – am I –

When "Landlords" turn the drunken Bee

Emily Dickinson

45.

Create a list of five books you've always wanted to read.

1

2

3

4

5

Learn how to juggle

46.

Hold two juggling balls in your right hand, one in the left.

Throw one right-hand ball up into a loop in front of you.

When it is at its peak, throw a second ball up — this one from your left hand.

Throw the third ball from your right as the second hits its peak — and as you catch the first.

Keep practising!

47.

Wordsearch.
Find all the slang terms for inebriation:

S	D	E	L	Z	Z	O	S	C
O	Y	S	P	I	T	W	L	D
U	M	R	R	Y	I	A	O	E
S	D	E	Z	Y	D	S	S	I
E	O	O	R	A	D	T	H	L
D	O	I	E	R	L	E	E	L
W	A	R	L	U	Y	D	D	O
L	E	G	L	E	S	S	A	R
D	D	E	L	D	D	A	L	T

48.

Now get creative!

Make up some of your own terms to describe your friends when they've had a few too many...

"carparked"   "gazeboed"

"panini'd?"

49.

Organise a stay-at-home
spa night.

Splash out on some face masks,
treatment oils, manicure sets,
etc, and invite friends round
for a DIY spa. Or all chip in and
hire a beautician to do the
pampering for you.

51.

Test out your balance with this challenge:

Take off your shoes and put your hands on your hips.

Lift one foot and rest it on the inside knee of your supporting leg.

Raise the heel of your supporting foot (the one still on the floor) so that you are standing on tiptoes.

The test ends when your hands move from your hips, the supporting foot moves position or the non-supporting foot moves from your knee.

How did you do?

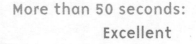

More than 50 seconds:
Excellent

40—50 seconds:
Good

25—39 seconds:
Average

10—24 seconds:
Fair

Less than 10 seconds:
Are you sure you haven't been drinking?

52.

Write a message
in a bottle:

To whoever finds this note…

53.

Baffle friends with this word puzzle:

"A blind beggar had a brother who died."

What relation was the blind beggar to the brother who died?

...and no, the answer isn't "brother"

Answer: sister (most people assume the "blind beggar" is male)

54.

Celebrate having hung up your beer goggles with this mindful observation exercise.

Choose a natural object in your line
of vision (anything from a cloud to a
blade of grass) and look at it for a full
minute, making sure you really notice
everything about what you are seeing.

55.

Create a pie chart
of your life.

On the blank chart opposite,
break down your daily routine
into what takes up most of
your mental energy.

Is there anything
you'd like to change?

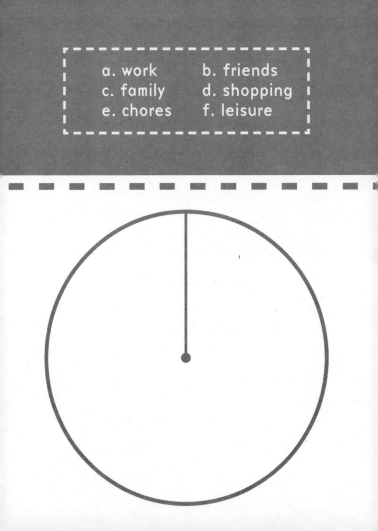

a. work   b. friends
c. family   d. shopping
e. chores   f. leisure

56.

Challenge your friends to a photo competition.

Arrange to meet up somewhere, then send everyone off for a ten-minute walk during which they must each take an "interesting" photograph.

Come back together and compare your shots.

57.

Add this mocktail to your party menu:

Pomegranate Mojito Mocktail

- 2 parts pomegranate juice
- 1 part lemonade
- A few fresh mint leaves, crushed
- A quarter of a lime

58.

Write down your favourite song lyrics about drinking.

_____

_____

_____

_____

_____

_____

59.

Revisit a place from your childhood.

What memories does it bring back?

60.

Host a potluck dinner.

Tell your guests to bring a dish of their choice but not reveal what it will be. Then enjoy a feast of strange combinations like sushi with lasagne and chocolate brownies.

61.

Wake up early and watch the sunrise.

62.

Give your brain a workout by solving this riddle:

A ship in a calm harbour has a ladder hanging over its side, the bottom rung of which just touches the water.

The distance between the rungs is 20cm and the length of the ladder is 180cm.

The tide is rising at a rate of 15cm each hour. How long will it take for the water to reach the seventh rung of the ladder?

A: Never. The boat, and ladder, will rise with the tide.

63.

Write down three things you keep putting off.

1

2

3

Either do them today or throw the list away.

64.

Throw a wild-flower
seed bomb at a place
that looks like it needs
more colour.

Go back from time to time
**and watch the
flowers grow.**

65.

Show off your sobriety by keeping
within the lines when you
colour in this
stress-busting design:

66.

Can you match up the Shakespeare play with the quotes opposite?

1. As You Like It: Act 3, Scene 5

2. Henry V: Act 3, Scene 2

3. The Merry Wives of Windsor: Act 1, Scene 1

4. Othello: Act 2, Scene 3

5. Macbeth: Act 2, Scene 3

a) "I would give all my fame for a pot of ale."

b) "Why, sir, for my part I say the gentleman had drunk himself out of his five senses."

c) "Drink, sir, is a great provoker of three things... nose painting, sleep and urine. Lechery, sir, it provokes, and unprovokes; it provokes the desire but takes away the performance."

d) "I pray you, do not fall in love with me, for I am falser than vows made in wine."

e) "O thou invisible spirit of wine! If thou hast no name to be known by, let us call thee devil!"

67.

Grab a smartphone and some friends and venture out on a GPS geocache hunt.

68.

Live stream a fitness class.

69.

Learn to play "House of the Rising Sun" on guitar.

The page opposite
shows you how.

e, B, G, D, A or E
=
which string to pluck

1, 2, 3, or 0 (for open string)
=
which fret to press

Go on, it's easy!

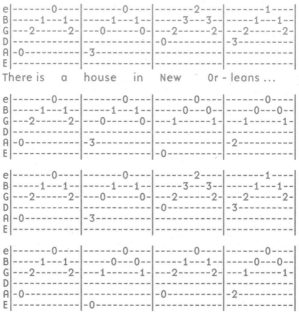

70.

Take a walk in the woods.

71.

Make a photo album of treasured pictures.

Don't just do a digital edit of your jpegs: get printing and put together an "actual" album, so that when you've finished you can hold it in your hands and flick through its pages.

72.

There was an Old Man of Apulia,

Whose conduct was very peculiar;

He fed twenty sons

Upon nothing but buns,

That whimsical man of Apulia.

— Edward Lear
A Book of Nonsense

Finish off the limerick on
the page opposite in the
style of Edward Lear:

My limerick

There was a young man from Derby

Author: _____

Date: _____

For the next week

take the stairs

instead of the

lift whenever

you can.

73.

74.

Start a dream journal.

taking an exam in your underwear

turning invisible

late for your flight

running but not moving

flying into space

performing on stage without lines

eating spaghetti

chasing butterflies

teeth falling out

75.

Give up some time for a good cause.

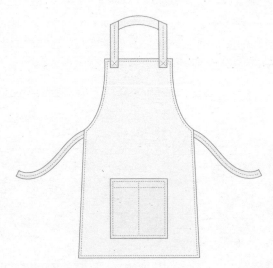

How about putting your name on a volunteer database?

76.

Write a letter to your future grandchildren.

Tell them about the world as it is today.

77.

Make a list of your five best sober nights out.

1

2

3

4

5

78.

Give yourself
a digital detox.

Spend a whole day with your
smartphone, computer and
games console switched off.

79.

Go to the beach

...regardless of the
time of year.

80.

Learn this magic trick to wow your friends:

The AMAZING Pre-sliced Banana!

Take a pin and make a series of holes along a banana.

Put the pin into each of the holes and carefully move it backwards and forwards to 'slice' the banana while it's still inside the skin.

The banana will look untouched from the outside but when you peel it it will be ready-sliced.

Ta-Da!

81.

Head into
town, find
somewhere
to sit and
simply watch
the world
go by.

82.

Host a dry book club.

Decide who you'll invite and what books you will recommend:

Participants:

....

....

....

....

Books:

(e.g. *After the Flood, Everything is Illuminated, Freedom?*)

....

....

....

....

83.

Master a new skill.

Go for something unexpected
like knitting or DJing
...or, er, taxidermy.

84.

Go to a sporting
event and cheer
for both sides.

85.

Walk around the rooms in your home and look at each one as if you were a stranger.

Is there anything you'd like to freshen up?

86.

Do 60 seconds of high intensity training.

Push ups, star jumps, sprinting or skipping — boost your fitness with a quick micro-routine.

87.

Visit the Tourist Information Centre closest to you and do two things suggested in the "local attractions" section.

88.

"But thanks be to God, since my leaving drinking of wine, I do find myself much better and do mind my business better."
— Samuel Pepys Diary
29 January 1662

Follow in Pepys' footsteps and keep a daily journal.

Start your first entry on the page opposite...

89.

Take a different route home from work.

Who knows what you will find...

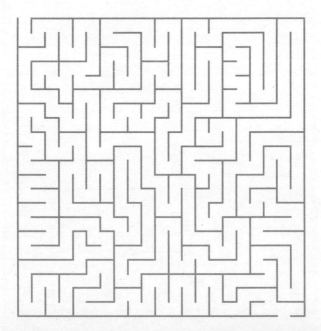

90.

Arrange a sober karaoke night.

You may think you sound like Beyoncé or Frank Sinatra after a few beers but now it's time to discover the power of your true inner voice.

91.

Think back to your teenage self. What three things needn't you have worried about?

1.

2.

3.

92.

Join a dance class

and prepare by learning
these basic waltz steps.

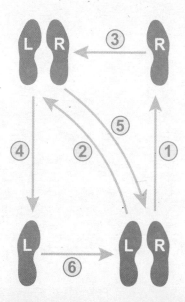

93.

Draw a cryptic treasure map on the page opposite, then cut out the page and leave it somewhere for someone to find...

94.

Look back on your life so far. Do you have a Sliding Doors moment?

Can you identify a point in time when you could have taken a different fork in the road? Do you think fate played its part?

95.

Which people in your life do you think best match these literary character descriptions?

"Looking at her, you got the feeling that this was someone who could bend iron bars and tear telephone directories in half."

of Miss Trunchbull
from Roald Dahl's *Matilda*

"Even though he had a Very Small Heart, it could hold a rather large amount of Gratitude."

of Piglet
from AA Milne's *Winnie the Pooh*

"A squeezing, wrenching, grasping, scraping, clutching, covetous, old sinner!"

of Ebenezer Scrooge
from Charles Dickens's *A Christmas Carol*

"She had a lively, playful disposition, which delighted in any thing ridiculous."

of Elizabeth Bennet
from Jane Austen's *Pride and Prejudice*

"His face is like a blade, and a knife, and a flicker of light: it is delicate and fierce, and scowls beautifully forever."

of Ben Gant
from Thomas Woolf's *Look Homeward, Angel*

"She will outstrip all praise and make it halt behind her."

of Miranda
from William Shakespeare's *The Tempest*

Gather some friends together for a game of laser tag.

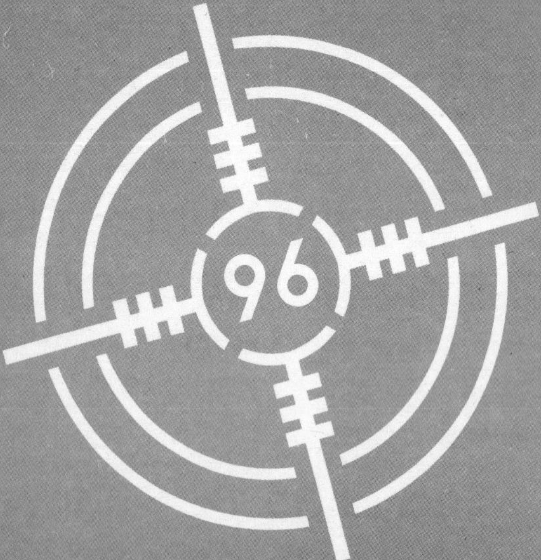

97.

A Drinking Song

Wine comes in at the mouth

And love comes in at the eye;

That's all we shall know for truth

Before we grow old and die.

I lift the glass to my mouth,

I look at you, and I sigh.

William Butler Yeats

98.

If you're missing late night visits to the kebab shop, try creating your own healthy kebab at home.

Here's a recipe:

Ingredients:

- 6 cloves of garlic
- 120ml lemon juice
- 60ml canola oil
- ½ teaspoon ground allspice
- ¼ teaspoon ground cinnamon
- Pinch of salt
- Pepper to taste
- 1kg cubed lamb steak
- 2 onions, cut into wedges

To make the marinade:

Crush the garlic and mix with the lemon juice, oil, allspice, cinnamon, salt and pepper.

Coat the meat. Cover and refrigerate for at least 2 hours...

For the kebab:

Preheat the grill to high.

Divide the lamb and onions between 6 skewers, brushing the onions with the remaining marinade.

Grill the kebabs for around 6 minutes on each side, depending on how you like your meat.

For that really authentic post-pub feel, put the kebab in pitta with some finely sliced iceberg lettuce and a splash of hot sauce.

99.

Arm yourself with these useful retorts for when you are next pressed to have a drink:

"Er... is that a vegan drink?"

"It plays havoc with my ankles."

"I don't agree with hanging on to dated imperialist dogma which perpetuates the economic and social differences in our society. If there is ever going to be any progress..."

100.

Write three positive statements about yourself as a non-drinker:

I am

I am

I am

101.

Now that you've seen the joys of a life without alcohol, write a haiku about anything you like:

Remember, a haiku doesn't have to rhyme and is made up of three lines of five, seven and five syllables